THE SUPER BOWL

by Tyler Omoth

CAPSTONE PRESS
a capstone imprint

Capstone Captivate is published by Capstone Press, an imprint of Capstone.
1710 Roe Crest Drive
North Mankato, Minnesota 56003
www.capstonepub.com

Copyright © 2020 by Capstone. All rights reserved. No part of this publication may be reproduced in whole or in part, or stored in a retrieval system, or transmitted in any form or by any means, electronic, mechanical, photocopying, recording, or otherwise, without written permission of the publisher.

Library of Congress Cataloging-in-Publication Data is available on the Library of Congress website.
ISBN: 978-1-5435-9191-0 (hardcover)
ISBN: 978-1-4966-5781-7 (paperback)
ISBN: 978-1-5435-9198-9 (eBook PDF)

Summary:
Discover the surprising facts, amazing stories, and legendary players of the Super Bowl.

Image Credits
Associated Press: 7, 14, Andrew Innerarity, 29, John Gapps III, 17, NFL Photos, 8, Tony Tomsic, 9, Vernon Biever, 15; Dreamstime: Jerry Coli, 16, Mbr Images, 18, 19, Tomatika, 12; Newscom: ABA, cover, Icon SMI, 23, Image of Sport/Steve Jacobson, 20, Reuters/Lucy Nicholson, 26, Reuters/Ray Stubblebine, 25, SuperChrome/Tony Tomsic, 13, ZUMA Press/Elizabeth Flores, 5, ZUMA Press/Scott A. Miller, 10; Shutterstock: EFKS, 1

Design Elements: Shutterstock

Editorial Credits
Editor: Gena Chester; Designer: Sarah Bennett; Media Researcher: Eric Gohl; Premedia Specialist: Spencer Rosio

All internet sites appearing in back matter were available and accurate when this book was sent to press.

Printed and bound in the USA.
PA99

Table of Contents

INTRODUCTION
The Philly Special 4

CHAPTER 1
History of the Super Bowl 6

CHAPTER 2
Great Teams 12

CHAPTER 3
Super Bowl Heroes 22

Glossary 30
Read More 31
Internet Sites 31
Index 32

Glossary terms are **bold** on first use.

INTRODUCTION

The Philly Special

Thirty-eight seconds remained in the first half of the 53rd Super Bowl, or Super Bowl LII. The Philadelphia Eagles led the New England Patriots by three points. The Eagles lined up at the Patriots' 2-yard line.

As quarterback Nick Foles called the play, he left his position behind the center. After Foles moved toward the right end of the Eagles' line, the center snapped the ball to the waiting running back.

The running back ran to the left. He flipped the ball to a wide receiver running the other way. The wide receiver fired a pass to Foles in the **end zone**. They scored a **touchdown**. The play is now called The Philly Special. It helped the Eagles beat the Patriots to win Super Bowl LII 41–33.

FAST FACT!
Only three quarterbacks have caught a touchdown pass in Super Bowl history. They were Foles, John Elway, and Jim Kelly.

Eagles quarterback Nick Foles catches a touchdown pass from tight end Trey Burton.

CHAPTER 1

History of the Super Bowl

The history of the Super Bowl goes back to the 1960s. There were two pro-football leagues in action at the time. One was the National Football League (NFL), and the other was the American Football League (AFL). Teams from the two leagues did not play each other. Each league crowned its own champion.

In 1966, officials from the NFL and AFL decided to join together. They agreed to form one league with two **conferences** by 1969. They also decided the top team from each league would play at the end of the 1966 season. It would be the first time the two leagues would face each other on the field. This game was the first Super Bowl.

Dolphins safety Bob Petrella intercepts a pass during an AFL game in 1967.

The Two Leagues

The NFL got its start about 100 years ago in 1920. The AFL wasn't created until 1959. The new league competed with the NFL. The AFL had its own star athletes and even its own TV deal. But the NFL had more money and its own set of stars. The two leagues did not get along. But in the end, they decided to come together to support the overall success of pro football.

At the first championship game, the Kansas City Chiefs of the AFL played the Green Bay Packers of the NFL. The game was named "AFL-NFL World Championship Game." They played in Los Angeles, California. The Packers won the game 35–10. Packers quarterback Bart Starr won the Most Valuable Player Award.

Packers running back Donny Anderson runs upfield against the Kansas City Chiefs in Super Bowl I. At the time, the Packers had played in the NFL for 49 seasons.

Packers defenders Willie Davis (right) and Henry Jordan (left) tackle Chiefs quarterback Len Dawson.

The owner of the Kansas City Chiefs started calling the AFL-NFL Championship Game the "Super Bowl." Sportswriters at the time liked the nickname. They used it. In 1969, "Super Bowl" became the game's formal title.

Steelers defenseman James Harrison catches a pass and runs a record 100 yards. The Steelers beat the Cardinals 27–23 to win Super Bowl XLII.

In 1970, the two leagues came together to form the new NFL. It had two conferences, the American Football Conference (AFC) and the National Football Conference (NFC). Today, each conference has 16 teams. Each conference is split into four **divisions**. Those divisions have four teams each.

Every season, six teams from each conference go to the playoffs. These teams are the four division winners and two **wild card** teams. Three rounds of games decide a winning team in each conference. Those two teams play each other in the Super Bowl.

In all its history, the Super Bowl has had come-from-behind wins and surprise teams. There have been a few powerful teams that have won several Super Bowls in just a few years.

FAST FACT!
The New England Patriots and Pittsburgh Steelers are tied for the most Super Bowl wins. Each team has six wins.

CHAPTER 2

Great Teams

1960s: Green Bay Packers

The Green Bay Packers were a great team years before they won Super Bowl I. Led by Hall-of-Fame coach Vince Lombardi, they won three NFL Championships and the first two Super Bowls during the 1960s.

Quarterback Bart Starr picked apart defenses with his strong arm. And on Packer defense, Ray Nitschke and Willie Davis made it difficult for other teams to score.

The Vince Lombardi Trophy

Every year the winning Super Bowl team gets the Vince Lombardi Trophy. It was originally called the Super Bowl Trophy. The name changed in 1971, a year after Lombardi died. The trophy looks like a football on a stand or how a football is set up for a kick.

Packers quarterback Bart Starr gets ready to fire a pass in Super Bowl I. Starr won the MVP award at both Super Bowl I and Super Bowl II.

1972–1980: Pittsburgh Steelers

The NFL in the 1970s belonged to the Pittsburgh Steelers. Head coach Chuck Knoll built a team filled with great players. Quarterback Terry Bradshaw and running back Franco Harris led a good, but simple **offense**. But the real stars of the 1970s Steelers played on **defense**.

In 1975, the Steelers defeated the Minnesota Vikings 16–6 to win Super Bowl IX.

Steelers running back Franco Harris runs upfield against Dallas Cowboys defenders. Steelers defeated the Cowboys 21–17 in Super Bowl X in 1976.

The defense was so strong it became known as the "Steel Curtain." The star players were "Mean" Joe Greene, Dwight White, Ernie Holmes, L. C. Greenwood, and Jack Lambert. They played hard and out-muscled other teams. It was one of the best defenses in NFL history. The "Steel Curtain" helped the Steelers win four Super Bowls between 1975 and 1980.

1981–1994: San Francisco 49ers

The San Francisco 49ers of the 1980s and early 1990s played football differently. Instead of being the strongest and the toughest team, they were the smartest.

Head coach Bill Walsh started a new style of offense. The "West Coast Offense" used short, quick passes to make a fast game. Defenses could not keep up.

Quarterbacks Joe Montana and Steve Young threw the ball well. One of the NFL's all-time best wide receivers, Jerry Rice, stayed busy catching the ball.

Quarterback Joe Montana took the 49ers to the Super Bowl four years in a row. He helped his team win each of those four games.

Jerry Rice celebrates after a touchdown in Super Bowl XXIV. Rice was added to the NFL Hall of Fame in 2010.

From 1981–1994, the 49ers had at least 10 wins each season. They made it to the playoffs 12 times and won five Super Bowls.

1992–1996: Dallas Cowboys

The Cowboys won big in the 1990s. It didn't last long, but it was still impressive. From 1992 to 1996, the Cowboys went to three Super Bowls and won all of them.

Coach Jimmy Johnson had a powerful offensive team. Troy Aikman was one of the best passers in the NFL. Michael Irvin was a big wide receiver and great hands and speed to catch passes from Aikman. At running back, Emmitt Smith used his speed to score points. He ran for more yards than any running back in history.

The Cowboys used a mix of runs and passes that could win and win big. In Super Bowl XXVII, they beat the Buffalo Bills by a score of 52–17. They won each of their three Super Bowls by at least 10 points.

Troy Aikman attempts a pass in Super Bowl XXX. Aikman played with the Cowboys from 1989 to 2000.

Cowboys quarterback Troy Aikman hands the ball to running back Emmitt Smith. Smith won the MVP award for Super Bowl XXVIII.

Patriots quarterback Tom Brady throws a pass in Super Bowl LIII. The Patriots went on to beat the Rams 13–3.

2001–2019: New England Patriots

No team in NFL history has had a period of success that has lasted as long as the New England Patriots. During an 18-year period beginning in 2001, the Patriots reached the Super Bowl nine times. They have won it six times.

Head coach Bill Belichick and quarterback Tom Brady led the team. The names and faces around Brady changed over they years. But they were almost always a winning group. The Patriots played strong on both sides of the ball and focused on key skills. This focus on the field produced amazing results.

FAST FACT!

Tom Brady has six Super Bowl rings—more than any other player. He also has the most Super Bowl MVP awards. He has won it four times.

CHAPTER 3

Super Bowl Heroes

The Guarantee

In the matchup between the New York Jets and the Baltimore Colts, everyone thought the Colts would win. But Jets quarterback Joe Namath was flashy and sure of himself. Three days before Super Bowl III, Namath told reporters the Jets would win.

His words became front page news. Namath's promise added pressure on the Jets to beat the Colts. In the game, Namath kept his word. He did not throw a touchdown pass, but he played well. He led the Jets to a 16–7 victory. He is the only Super Bowl MVP quarterback who didn't throw for a touchdown.

Colts quarterback Joe Namath drops back to throw a pass in Super Bowl III. In 1985, Namath was added into the Pro Football Hall of Fame.

The Tackle

There were six seconds left in Super Bowl XXXIV. The St. Louis Rams were leading the Tennessee Titans 23–16. The Titans lined up at the Rams' 10-yard line. The Titans had one last shot to score a touchdown to tie the game.

The Titans' quarterback was Steve McNair. He fired a pass to wide receiver Kevin Dyson, who cut across the middle of the field. Dyson would have scored easily if not for linebacker Mike Jones.

Jones stopped the speedy receiver. Dyson tried to reach the ball into the end zone, but it was no use. Jones's perfect tackle left him inches short. The game was over. "The Tackle" was the last play of a great Super Bowl. The Rams escaped with the win.

Rams linebacker Mike Jones stops Titans wide receiver Kevin Dyson at the one-yard line. Jones had suffered an ankle injury in the third quarter, but he powered through to the end of the game to make his famous tackle.

Giants receiver David Tyree (right) completes an amazing catch in Super Bowl XLII. Tyree had to compete with Patriots defender Rodney Harrison (left).

The Helmet Catch

The New England Patriots faced the New York Giants in Super Bowl XLII. Late in the game the Patriots led the Giants 14–10. There was only 1 minute and 16 seconds left to play. The Giants had the ball but struggled to move down field. On third down, Giants' quarterback Eli Manning escaped the defense. He threw a pass to receiver David Tyree. The ball sailed high. Tyree jumped up to catch it.

The ball almost slipped through Tyree's hands. Somehow he pinned it against his helmet. He held it there as he fell to the turf. It was a 32-yard gain for the Giants. Four plays later, the Giants scored a touchdown and won the game. The Patriots had lost for the first time in their entire season.

The Arrival

It's never easy for a new player to follow one of the all-time greats. When Joe Montana left the San Francisco 49ers, Steve Young took over at quarterback.

In Super Bowl XXIX, Young led the 49ers past the San Diego Chargers by a score of 49–26. He passed for 325 yards and ran for 49 yards. He became the first player to lead a game in both passing and rushing. He also broke a Super Bowl record by throwing six touchdown passes. It was one of the best games by a quarterback in Super Bowl history.

49ers quarterback Steve Young runs over Chargers cornerback Darrien Gordon. Young received the MVP award for Super Bowl XXIX.

Glossary

conference (KAHN-fuhr-uhns)—a grouping of sports teams that play against each other

defense (di-FENS)—the team that tries to stop points from being scored

division (duh-VI-zhuhn)—a group of teams in a conference

end zone (END ZOHN)—the area between the goal line and the end line at either end of a football field

offense (aw-FENSS)—the team that has the ball and is trying to score

touchdown (TUCH-down)—a play in football in which a team carries the ball into the opponent's end zone for six points

wild card (WILD CARD)—a team that advances to the playoffs without winning its division

Read More

Blaine, Richard. *Cups, Bowls, and Other Football Championships.* New York: Crabtree Publishing Company, 2016.

Braun, Eric. *Super Bowl Records.* North Mankato, MN: Capstone Press, a Capstone imprint, 2017.

Frederick, Shane. *The Super Bowl's Greatest Plays.* North Mankato, MN: Capstone Press, a Capstone imprint, 2017.

Internet Sites

The NFL Play 60 Movement
www.nfl.com/play60

Sports Illustrated Kids
www.sikids.com/football

Super Bowl News
www.nfl.com/super-bowl

Index

Baltimore Colts, 22
Buffalo Bills, 18

Dallas Cowboys, 18
    Aikman, Troy, 18
    Irvin, Michael, 18
    Johnson, Jimmy, 18
    Smith, Emmitt, 18

Green Bay Packers, 8, 12
    Davis, Willie, 12
    Lombardi, Vince, 12
    Nitschke, Ray, 12
    Starr, Bart, 8, 12

Kansas City Chiefs, 8, 9

New England Patriots, 4, 11, 21, 27
    Belichick, Bill, 21
    Brady, Tom, 21
New York Giants, 27
    Manning, Eli, 27
    Tyree, David, 27
New York Jets, 22
    Namath, Joe, 22

Philadelphia Eagles, 4
    Foles, Nick, 4
    Philly Special, the, 4

Pittsburgh Steelers, 11, 14
    Bradshaw, Terry, 14
    Greene, Joe, 15
    Greenwood, L. C., 15
    Harris, Franco, 14
    Holmes, Ernie, 15
    Knoll, Chuck, 14
    Lambert, Jack, 15
    Steel Curtain, the, 15
    White, Dwight, 15

San Diego Chargers, 28
San Francisco 49ers, 16, 28
    Montana, Joe, 16, 28
    Rice, Jerry, 16
    Walsh, Bill, 16
    West Coast Offense, 16
    Young, Steve, 16, 28
St. Louis Rams, 24
    Dyson, Kevin, 24
    Jones, Mike, 24

Tennessee Titans, 24
    McNair, Steve, 24